June 2025.

Andrew,

The love of my ey......

Always yours,

Debbie

— x —

Worlds
of
Affirmation

100 expressions of love from around the globe

Ella Wrenwood

Worlds
of
Affirmation

100 expressions of love from around the globe

Ella Wrenwood

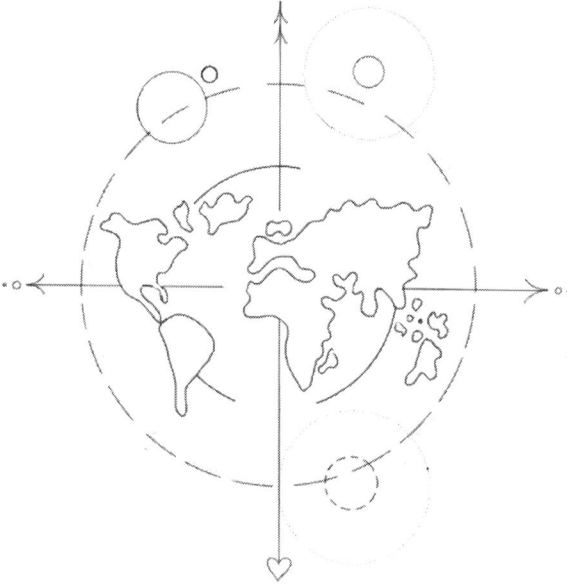

No matter where you are in the world, this is for you:

This book is a passport to love in all its forms — 100 words, proverbs, and sayings that capture what English never quite could. Here, you'll find devotion in Arabic, longing in Portuguese, butterflies in Tagalog, and so much more.

Whether you bought this book for yourself or received it as a gift, you'll discover how different cultures describe love, not just in words, but in the way they live, cherish, and express it — a reminder that love, in all its forms, is universal.

Conservative estimates say we learn 5–8 new words a day when picking up a language, so that's my recommendation to you here: take it slow. Savor a few pages at a time. But of course, you're welcome to wander through this book however you like.

Because whether you're learning a new phrase or hearing an old feeling put into words for the first time, I hope every page reminds you of a simple truth:

Love is vast, limitless, and always worth exploring.

Let's begin.

.

Love understands all languages.

— Romanian proverb

Ikigai

Japanese

The secret to a long and happy life?

In Japan, there's a word called *ikigai* — a blend of *iki*, meaning "to live," and *gai*, meaning "reason."

It translates to "a reason to live." Ikigai is all about finding what truly matters to you — what gets you out of bed each morning with purpose and joy.

Some people spend their whole lives searching for it, but I already know mine.

It's you. You are my ikigai.

Jaan

Hindi/Urdu/Farsi

Sometimes, I feel like there are no words to describe how much you mean to me.

But then, there are words like *jaan* — a Hindi, Urdu, and Farsi term of endearment that means "life," "soul," or "darling." You can also say "meri jaan," which means "my life."

Jaan is also a name of Persian origin meaning "soul" or "life," and it can even be added to other names to make them sweeter, more intimate — like a whispered "dear."

Dear. Darling. Life. Soul.

Yeah, I guess that just about sums you up.

Hai shi shan meng
Chinese

When I say I want to be with you forever, I mean *hai shi shan meng*.

Hai shi shan meng is a Chinese idiom that means to pledge undying love — a promise as enduring as the sea and mountains.

It's a vow sworn on the *hai*, the oceans that stretch endlessly, and the *shan*, the mountains that stand immovable through time.

And for me, it's not just a saying; it's true.

The seas could dry up, the mountains could crumble, and I would still love you.

Cheiro no cangote

[Portuguese] *verb*

To gently nuzzle your lover's neck with the tip of your nose.

Dor

Romanian

When you're gone, I feel *dor.*

Dor is a Romanian word with no English equivalent. It most closely resembles "longing" or "yearning," but it also carries layers of joy, melancholy, passion, and nostalgia — a soul-deep ache for something cherished yet just out of reach.

And yet, despite all that, dor misses one thing:

viraha, the Hindi word that describes "the realization of love through separation."

Because when you're gone, it's not just the ache or the longing or any of the other emotions — it's the depth of my love for you growing.

That's what I feel.

Mahal kita
Tagalog

"I love you" is sweet, but *mahal kita* says so much more.

Mahal kita is a Filipino expression that means "I love you," but it also holds a deeper meaning.

Mahal literally translates to "expensive," but in the context of love, it means "precious" or "priceless."

To call someone "mahal" is to say they're valuable beyond measure. And for you, that couldn't be truer.

You're the most precious thing in my life.

And your love? *Priceless.*

Cwtch

Welsh

Let's *cwtch*.

Pronounced "kutch," like "butch," cwtch is a Welsh word for a cuddle or hug — not just any hug, though.

It's a hug that wraps you up completely, a safe little bubble where nothing else matters. A cuddle that shields you from the world and says, "You're loved, you're safe, you're home."

And that's what you are to me.

My home. My heart. My cwtch.

"Love is of all the passions the strongest, for it attacks simultaneously the head, the heart, and the senses."

— Lao Tzu, Chinese philosopher and founder of Taoism

Tsundoku

Japanese

In Japanese, *tsundoku* means collecting books and letting them pile up unread — not for neglect, but for the joy of knowing they're there, full of untold stories.

In a way, loving you feels like my own tsundoku. I'm constantly collecting memories — laughs, glances, whispers, kisses — that pile up in my heart, like a library of us.

And just like those books, I'll never get tired of revisiting them. Because with you, every moment is a story worth keeping.

Flâner

French

I have an idea for our next day out:

Let's *flâner* — a French word that means to stroll without a destination, savoring the beauty of the moment and the world around us.

We'd wander into little cafes, explore hidden streets, and talk about everything and nothing

We'd laugh until our cheeks hurt, hold hands without a reason, and act like big kids for a few hours.

No phones. No distractions. Just us — seeing, hearing, and feeling everything, together.

Ya'aburnee
Arabic

In Arabic, they don't say "I love you," they say *ya'aburnee*.

It translates to "you bury me," meaning "when the time comes, I hope I go before you, because I couldn't imagine living without you."

I know we're a long way off, and I know we have many memories left to make, but the sentiment remains:

A world without you is no world at all.

Manja

[Malay] *noun*

A person who shows so much outward love and affection towards someone, to the point where they are pampering or spoiling them.

Kỳ diệu

Vietnamese

Some words feel like little miracles themselves — like *kỳ diệu*.

Kỳ diệu is a Vietnamese word that means "wondrous" or "magical." It describes the rush of excitement when you stumble upon something new, and the joy that multiplies when you share that discovery with someone you love.

Since meeting you, I feel kỳ diệu all the time.

Whether it's learning something new about you, seeing the world through your eyes, or discovering things about myself I didn't even know, every moment with you feels like a little miracle.

Onsra

Boro

In the Boro language of India, the word *onsra* means "to love for the last time."

It's a word for the kind of love where two people know it's coming to an end. A love in its final stages, fading like the last embers of a fire.

But for you and I, onsra means something entirely different.

You're the last love I'll ever know, not because I feel it's coming to an end, but because I *know* there will never be anyone else.

You're it for me — the beginning, the middle, and the love I'll carry to the end of my days.

Mi cielo
Spanish

"Sweetheart" is cute, "darling" is nice, and "baby" is okay and all.

But you're more than just words to me. You're *mi cielo.*

In Spanish, mi cielo means "my heaven" or "my sky." It's more than a term of endearment — it's a declaration of love so boundless it feels infinite.

A way of saying you're everything to me; the sky above me, the air I breathe, the horizon I always look for.

Put simply, it's the only phrase that even comes close to describing you.

Abhisar

[Bengali] noun

Lit. "going towards;" a secret meeting or rendezvous between two lovers.

Hubb
Arabic

There are countless words for "love" in Arabic, but *hubb* feels like it was made for us.

It comes from the same root as the word "seed;" something small, with the potential to grow into something beautiful.

Hubb reminds me of our story. What started as a seed has grown into something bigger, deeper, and more meaningful with each passing day.

Now, our love has branches that stretch toward the sky and roots that reach deep into my soul.

And you? You're my hubb — the seed that started it all.

Nepakartojama
Lithuanian

At times, I still can't believe you're mine.

I still can't believe how perfect you are.
I still can't believe you've chosen me.
And I still can't believe how lucky I am.

I guess we'll just have to call it a *nepakartojama*; a Lithuanian word for a perfect situation that will never happen again, literally "unable to repeat."

Meeting you was exactly that — a perfect, once-in-a-lifetime moment, never to be repeated.

Here, there, and everywhere

My perfect day with you?

Morning:
Go to the park and listen to *psithirisma* (the sound of the wind rustling through the leaves; *Greek*).

Afternoon:
Have a dip in the sea followed by *hanyauku* (to walk on tiptoes across warm sand; *Kwangali*).

Evening:
Dine at a romantic restaurant until we feel *abbiocco* (the pleasant drowsiness after eating a large meal; *Italian*).

Night:
Stay up late, lost in *samar* (those late-night talks that stretch long after the sun has set; *Arabic*).

And then? Well, that's up to you.

Merak
Serbian

They say it's the little things that matter most.

Especially in Serbia, where *merak* describes the bliss and sense of oneness with the universe found in life's simplest pleasures.

Merak can come from any small thing: enjoying a hot drink on a cold day, feeling the salt air on your face at the beach, or gazing up at a sky full of stars.

But for me, I feel it whenever I'm with you. I feel it when you laugh at my silly jokes, when you reach for my hand without thinking, and when you look at me like I'm the only person in the room.

Because the little things about you aren't little to me at all. They're *everything*.

Peiskos

[Norwegian] *noun*

The cozy feeling that comes from snuggling indoors in front of an open fire.

Odnoliub
Russian

There's something you need to know about me...

I'm an *odnoliub*.

In Russian, an odnoliub is "someone who only has one love in their life."

Some believe it means loving one person forever, even if they're no longer here. Others say it's about being able to love only one person or one thing at a time.

But for me, it means this:

Because I have you, no other love could ever compare. You're my one, my only, and my always.

Xìngfú

Chinese

When I say you make me happy, I'm talking about *xìngfú*.

The Chinese word xìngfú means "happiness" or "happy," but unlike other Chinese words for happiness, xìngfú carries a depth that sets it apart.

While kāixīn and kuàilè describe fleeting joy, xìngfú is different. It's a deep, lasting happiness that comes from a life filled with love, connection, and meaning.

The kind of happiness that grows in the presence of someone who loves you completely, where simply being together makes everything feel right.

That's what you've given me: not just moments of joy, but a lifetime of true happiness.

Gökotta
Swedish

Some things are worth waking up early for.

1. Seeing you sleeping next to me.

2. Watching the first light touch your skin.

3. *Gökotta.*

Gökotta is a Swedish word that means "rising at dawn to listen to bird song." It's about waking up early, experiencing the stillness of the morning, and finding gratitude in the beauty of nature.

That's the kind of morning I want, always — just you, me, and the world waking up around us.

"The more I think it over, the more I feel that there is nothing more truly artistic than to love people."

— Vincent van Gogh, Dutch painter

Aloha
Hawaiian

Did you know that *aloha* means more than just "hello" in Hawaiian?

Its literal translation is "the presence of breath" or "the breath of life," with *alo* meaning presence and *ha* meaning breath.

But it's more than that, too. Aloha is the foundation of Hawaiian values: love, affection, generosity, patience, and listening to others.

It feels fitting, doesn't it? Because those are the values we share, too.

So to my heart, my soul, my every breath: *Aloha no au ia `oe* (I truly love you).

Ⲣⲉϥⲉⲣⲟⲩⲱⲓⲛⲓ
Bohairic Coptic

Have you ever seen something so beautiful you couldn't put it into words?

In Turkish, *yakamoz* describes the moonlight as it dances on the water at night, loosely translating to "sea sparkle."

In Japanese, *komorebi* refers to rays of light dappling through overhead leaves, literally "sunlight leaking through trees."

But my favorite comes from Bohairic Coptic, an ancient Egyptian language: Ⲣⲉϥⲉⲣⲟⲩⲱⲓⲛⲓ (ref-er-oo-oi-nee), meaning "one who gives light."

Because that's what you are to me — the one who brings light to my life.

Mo chuisle, mo chroí
Irish

You're more than my other half, you're *mo chuisle, mo chroí.*

Mo chuisle, mo chroí (moh cooish-lah moh kree) is an Irish phrase that means "my pulse, my heart" — or more figuratively, "my darling."

For you, though, I think I prefer the literal translation.

You are my pulse, my heartbeat. And I couldn't live without you.

Ullassa

[Sanskrit] *noun*

Feelings of joy and pleasantness associated with natural beauty.*

*Do I even need to explain this one?

Kjæreste

Norwegian

Did you know that in Norway, they don't have a word for boyfriend or girlfriend?

Instead, they have *kjæreste*, which translates to "dearest one."

I can't think of a better word for you, because you really are the dearest person in my life.

Livsnjutare
Swedish

Before I met you, I was *lebensmüde*.

Lebensmüde is a German word that combines *leben* (life) and *müde* (tired), meaning "life-tired."

But now that I have you, I'm a *livsnjutare*.

In Swedish, livsnjutare means someone who loves life deeply; someone who savors every moment and finds joy in every season of life.

In other words, you didn't just change my world — *you gave it back to me.*

Koi no yokan
Japanese

Have you heard of *koi no yokan*?

It's a Japanese phrase that means "premonition of love" — the feeling upon first meeting someone that you will inevitably fall in love with them.

There's no direct English translation, but that's okay. I don't need one.

I felt it when I met you.

Házisárkány

[Hungarian] *noun*

"Domestic dragon," a playful and ironic nickname for a partner at home.

Drachenfutter

[German] *noun*

"Dragon fodder," a gift given to a spouse or partner after doing something wrong or foolish.

Hygge
Danish

You are my *hygge*.

Pronounced "hue-gah," hygge is a Danish concept that's all about finding happiness in life's little comforts and simple, cozy moments.

For some, it's the soft glow of candlelight, the weight of a thick blanket, or a warm fire on a cold winter's night.

But for me? It's you. Your smile, your voice, your touch, your hugs, your laugh, your eyes — even the quiet moments where you're just there.

Because you're not just part of my happiness; you *are* it.

Ahavah
Hebrew

In Hebrew, the word for love, *ahavah*, comes from the root word *hav*, which means "to give."

Ahavah says that love is an act of giving — not just gifts or gestures, but of yourself. Giving is said to bridge the space between souls, creating a connection so deep it feels like two souls becoming one.

It's a reminder that true love isn't about what you take, but what you give. So when I say "I love you," know that I mean this:

I ahavah you — I give myself to you, fully and freely, in every way I can.

Your happiness is mine. Your dreams are mine. But my love? *All yours.*

Milozvučan
Bosnian/Croatian/Serbian

Your voice is my favorite sound.

If I had to describe it in a word, it would be *milozvučan*.

Milozvučan is a Bosnian, Croatian, and Serbian word that means "sweetly-sounding." Originally used for those with beautiful singing voices, it's come to describe anyone with a voice that's gentle, warm, and soothing.

So please, keep talking, keep laughing, keep telling me all your stories, keep sharing your secrets, keep whispering your dreams in the dark, mumbling sleepy good mornings, and singing songs only we know.

I'll never get tired of listening to you.

Schnapsidee

German

I just had a *schnapsidee*.

It's a word from German bringing together *schnaps* (liquor) and *idee* (idea), meaning a wild or absurd idea, often (but not always) fueled by alcohol.

So forgive me if this sounds wild, but here's my idea:

Let's spend the rest of our lives together, drunk on love, chasing dreams, and making this crazy idea of forever a reality.

Cheers to that?

Ciğerpare

[Turkish] *noun*

A word of Persian origin meaning "liver part," used to express deep affection for someone you love as much as your own body.

Lovers or friends may say *ciğerparem*, meaning "my liver part."

Sobremesa

Spanish

You know that thing when you're at a restaurant, and the meal is finished but no one's in a rush to leave?

The outside world fades away, and all that's left is the soft glow of candles, conversation flowing freely, and the sound of laughter in the air.

The Spanish have a word for it — *sobremesa*.

And it's how I feel whenever I'm with you.

Suaimhneas croí

Gaelic

Suaimhneas croí (soo-iv-ness cree) is a Gaelic term for the state of happiness that comes from completing a task.

You might feel it after turning in a big project, putting the last piece into a puzzle, or finally fixing that thing at home you've been putting off for weeks.

For me though, I feel suaimhneas croí on an even deeper level — because I've completed the biggest task of all.

The task in question?

Finding you, my soulmate.

Wabi-sabi
Japanese

I used to think I wanted the perfect love story, but with you, I've discovered the beauty of *wabi-sabi.*

Wabi-sabi is a Japanese concept about finding beauty in imperfection — like dried flowers, aged wood, or kintsugi: the art of taking broken pottery and filling its cracks with gold.

I see wabi-sabi in you, too. In the way your hair falls into your eyes, in the crinkle in your nose when you laugh, or the little crease in your brow when you're lost in thought.

And it's not just the little things. I want to stand beside you on the hard days, love you through every flaw, and cherish every messy, imperfect moment.

Because I know now that true love doesn't have to be perfect — it just has to be ours.

"Lovers don't finally meet somewhere.
They're in each other all along."

— Rumi, Persian poet and Sufi mystic

Al-hawa
Arabic

Some forces in life are impossible to resist.

You were one of them.

In Arabic, attraction is considered the first stage of love. Known as *al-hawa*, it comes from the verb *hawa*, meaning "to blow."

Al-hawa tells us that love is like the wind — unavoidable, invisible, and capable of arriving out of nowhere.

And that's exactly what you did. You arrived without warning — one moment, a breeze; the next, a storm.

And me? *I never stood a chance.*

Trúnó
Icelandic

Have you heard of a *trúnó*?

It's an Icelandic word for those deep, meaningful conversations that happen late at night, usually with a drink in hand.

But with us, we don't need alcohol, and it doesn't matter what time of day it is. I know I can tell you my innermost thoughts, my secrets, and I'll always be safe with you.

Because every conversation with you is a trúnó.

Ayóó aníínishní'
Navajo

Did you know there's no direct word for "love" in Navajo?

Instead, they use *ayóó áníínishní,* which means "I have a regard for you."

It speaks to a deep reverence, an unshakable admiration, and a profound respect for the person you cherish.

So yes, I do love you. But ayóó áníínishní even more."

Kanyirninpa

[Kukatja/Aboriginal Pintupi] *noun*

Loosely translated as "holding," it describes an intimate embrace — one that conveys deep nurturance, protection, and an unspoken bond between the one who holds and the one who is held.

Desbundar

Portuguese

You know that feeling when you're somewhere new, and at first, you're a little unsure of yourself?

But as time goes on, you start to relax, and before you know it, you're completely at ease, wondering why you were even nervous in the first place?

The Portuguese call this *desbundar* — "to shed one's inhibitions in having fun."

You have that same effect on me. Whenever I'm with you, my nerves quiet, my mind softens, and I find myself having the best time without even trying.

With you, time doesn't just pass. It *disappears*.

Apapachar
Spanish

There's a word for the way you love me — *apapachar*.

It's a Spanish word that means "to caress with the soul," from the ancient Náhuatl *papachoa*, meaning to knead or massage with love.

That's what your love feels like to me. Your touch, your words, and even your presence are like a gentle embrace that reaches beyond my skin, straight to the soul.

I can only hope I make you feel the same way.

Yī rì sān qiū

Chinese

Being away from you feels like *yī rì sān qiū*.

Yī rì sān qiū is an ancient Chinese idiom that translates to "one day, three autumns."

It describes the aching slowness of time when you're apart from someone you love.

And for me, that someone is you.

Every moment without you feels like an eternity, but it only makes our reunions that much sweeter.

Like the first breath of spring.

Ya ruh al-ruh
Arabic

You're more than my soulmate. You're *ya ruh al-ruh*.

Ya ruh al-ruh is an Arabic phrase that means "soul of my soul."

While a soulmate feels like someone you're destined to meet, ya ruh al-ruh speaks to an eternal bond; two souls so deeply intertwined that they were never separate to begin with.

It's as if a part of me has always been in you, and a part of you in me, long before we found each other.

It's why I don't just feel connected to you — I feel *complete* with you.

Oodal

[Tamil] *noun*

A playful display of exaggerated anger to express affection, jealousy, or desire. Also refers to the melodramatic sulking after an argument between lovers, often used to nudge the other into apologizing.

Elmosolyodni
Hungarian

Picture it: someone tells you a joke. It's not even that funny, yet your lips curl into a small, involuntary smirk before breaking into a genuine smile.

The Hungarians have a word for this — *elmosolyodni*. Coming from *mosoly*, the word for smile, it captures those fleeting, uncontainable moments of happiness.

I don't know why, but something about you always gets to me. Whether you're telling me a joke, giving me a look from across the room, or simply crossing my mind, you always find a way to make me smile.

Sine qua non

Latin

In Latin, a *sine qua non* describes a necessary condition without which something is not possible — literally, "without which, not."

For example:

Water is the sine qua non of life.
A spark is the sine qua non of a fire.
And you are the sine qua non of me.

You've changed me in ways I never thought possible, giving me strength I didn't know I had, peace I'd forgotten how to feel, and a love I never imagined could be mine.

At the core of it all is one simple truth: there *is* no me without you.

Besa

Albanian

In Albanian society, *besa* means "to keep a promise." It's a cornerstone of their culture, symbolizing loyalty, trust, and a deep sense of responsibility to one's word. To give someone your besa is to make a solemn, inviolable oath.

So today, I borrow from that tradition to give you my besa: I promise to always keep my word, to stand by you through everything, and to be loyal to you forever.

I promise to see you, to hear you, and to love you exactly as you are.

And honestly, that's the easiest promise I've ever made.

"Love is born into every human being; it calls back the halves of our original nature together; it tries to make one out of two and heal the wound of human nature."

— Plato, Greek philosopher

Gigil
Tagalog

You make me *gigil*.

And no, that's not a typo — gigil is a Filipino term that describes the irresistible urge to pinch or squeeze something cute or adorable.

It's considered an untranslatable word for pure joy; like love spilling over, too big to keep inside.

So if I hold you a little too tight, or pull you a little too close, blame the gigil. I can't help it.

Ubuntu
Zulu

Have you ever heard of *ubuntu*?

Ubuntu is an African term that means "I am because we are," from the Zulu phrase *Umuntu ngumuntu ngabantu*, which literally means that a person is a person through other people.

At its core, ubuntu speaks to the idea that we are shaped by our relationships, that we grow, change, and become our best selves through the love and connection we share with others.

And that's precisely what you've done for me. You've softened my edges, strengthened my heart, and shared all the best parts of yourself with me

I guess what I'm really trying to say is this: *I am who I am because of you.* And because of that, I really, really love the person I've become.

Mysa

Swedish

My favorite thing to do with you?

Mysa.

In Swedish, mysa means "to cozy up" or "to snuggle," but it's more than that — it's the quiet joy of being completely at ease, savoring a moment of warmth and connection with someone you love.

It's that deep sense of belonging, knowing there's nowhere else you'd rather be, and no one else you'd rather be with.

And that's how I feel whenever I'm with you.

Ghalidan

[Persian] *verb*

To roll from side to side as lovers do.

Yuánfèn
Chinese

Do you believe in fate?

The Chinese word *yuánfèn* describes the belief that certain people are destined to meet, no matter how far apart they begin.

Unlike fate, yuánfèn is more like "fateful coincidence" — a predestined affinity that brings two people together, even if life has pulled them apart.

It's the idea that some connections are written in the stars, like two threads on opposite sides of the world, woven together by something greater than chance.

And somehow, in a world of 8 billion people, we found each other.

(Or maybe, just maybe, we were always meant to.)

Vedriti

Slovenian

To the strongest person I know:

In Slovenian, *vedriti* means to "take shelter from the rain," both in the literal sense and as a metaphor for finding refuge during difficult times.

So when the clouds feel like they're closing in and the rain won't let up, remember this: whatever storm you're facing, I'll be your shelter until it passes.

I'll be your safe space — the place you come to when the world feels heavy, whether it's for a few minutes, a few days, or for as long as you need.

Nothing would make me happier than to be that for you, because that's exactly what you are to me.

My shelter.

Il dolce far niente
Italian

Isn't it nice to just do nothing sometimes?

So nice in fact, that in Italy, they have a phrase for it: *il dolce far niente*, which means "the sweetness of doing nothing."

It's about slowing down, savoring the present, and embracing life without rushing to the next moment.

I didn't always understand it, but with you, I do.

Because with you, even the quiet moments feel full, even the ordinary feels extraordinary, and every "nothing" feels like everything.

Queesting

[Dutch] *verb*

To invite someone into your bed for intimate pillow talk.

Iktsuarpok

Inuit

You know that feeling when you're waiting for something or someone to arrive, and the anticipation is so intense that you keep checking the door to see if they're there?

The Inuit have a word for it — *iktsuarpok* — and it's exactly how I get about you.

Whether I'm checking my phone for your message, waiting by the door because I know you're on the way, or just counting down the minutes until I get to see you again, nothing excites me more knowing I'm about to see you.

Naz

Persian/Urdu

You don't just make me feel loved; you make me feel *naz*.

Naz is a word with mysterious origins, found across several languages influenced by Persian and Arabic. It holds different meanings depending on where it's spoken — from charm and grace to coy or coquettish.

But my favorite meaning comes from Urdu, where naz refers to "the pride you feel from being loved."

It's the perfect word for how you make me feel. Proud.

And I'll never stop being proud to call you mine.

Retrouvailles

French

In French, *retrouvailles* describes the irrepressible joy of reuniting with someone after a long time apart.

It's a beautiful word, but it doesn't quite work for you and I — specifically, the "long time" part.

Because I don't need time or distance. I feel it every morning when I roll over and see you lying next to me. I feel it every evening when you walk through the door. I even feel it when you leave the room for a few minutes and come back.

It's as if my heart can't tell the difference between five seconds and five years; only that it misses you.

"Intense love does not measure, it just gives."

— Mother Teresa, Albanian-Indian Catholic nun

Sabsung
Thai

Do you know how happy you make me?

Sabsung is a Thai word that describes the feeling of being revitalized — of something or someone bringing you back to life, like quenching a deep thirst (literally "immersing in liquid").

And for me, that someone was you.

Like cool water on a scorching day, you restored something in me. You filled a space I didn't even know was empty, turned exhaustion into energy, and made life feel lighter, brighter, fuller.

You are the breath of fresh air I didn't know I needed.

Donna mirai ni mo ai wa aru

Japanese

I may not know exactly what the future holds, but I do know one thing for sure:

Donna mirai ni mo ai wa aru.

This Japanese phrase means, "Whatever future there is, there is love."

It's a promise that has been shared across time — whispered by lovers parting at a train station, scribbled by childhood sweethearts vowing to meet again, or spoken by soulmates promising to endure, no matter what comes.

But for me, it means this:

Whatever future there is, I have you. And because I have you, there will *always* be love.

Yêu & Thương
Vietnamese

In Vietnamese, there are two main words to express love: *yêu* and *thương*.

Yêu is an intense, passionate love — the kind that sets your heart racing, often felt in the early stages of a relationship.

Thương, by contrast, is quieter and more enduring. It's a love rooted in care and responsibility, the kind that deepens over a lifetime together.

They describe different kinds of love, but for me, they both apply to you.

I thương you in all the ways that matter — the care, the commitment, the quiet acts of love. But I've never lost the yêu — the spark, the passion, the butterflies.

I yêu you *and* I thương you, and I always will.

Cafuné

[Portuguese] *verb*

To tenderly run your fingers through a lover's hair.

Forelsket
Norwegian

Did you know that in Norway, they don't have a word for "crush?"

Instead, they have *forelsket*, which describes the euphoria you feel when you first begin to fall in love.

It's that fluttery, heart-racing, palms-sweating feeling. Not just a crush, but an I-wanna-spend-the-rest-of-my-life-with-you kinda feeling.

That's what I felt when I first met you;
not just a spark, but the beginning of forever.

Geborgenheit

German

Geborgenheit is a German word that means more than just "security" or "safety." It's a deep sense of comfort, warmth, and belonging that's hard to put into words.

It could be the smell of a familiar meal that reminds you of home, the sound of a loved one's voice, or the steady rhythm of a heartbeat against your ear.

For me, though, it's simply being with you. It's the way I feel in your presence, in your arms, and in your love.

And it's my favorite feeling in the world.

Meraki
Greek

The reason we work so well together?

Meraki.

In Greek, meraki means to pour your heart and soul into something, leaving a piece of yourself behind (or "the essence of yourself").

Meraki is a mindset, a way of life, and a guiding principle reminding us to do everything with love and care.

It's why our relationship doesn't feel like effort, but a labor of love — because we both show up fully and wholeheartedly, with care, pride, and devotion.

With meraki, we've created something beautiful: a love that reflects the best parts of *both* of us.

Flechazo

[Spanish] *noun*

Originally referring to the wound caused by an arrow, flechazo is now commonly used to describe the sudden and intense moment when love strikes unexpectedly.

Kilig

Tagalog

Some words don't need a translation; you just know it when you feel it.

Kilig is one of those words. A Tagalog term with no direct English equivalent, it's that fluttery, excited feeling you get in your chest when you feel love, like a shiver of happiness.

I may not be able to define it, but I feel it. Every time you look at me. Every time you touch me. Every time you say my name.

And if I could bottle the feeling, I'd keep it with me forever.

Samvær

Danish

There's a word in Danish, *samvær*, that means simply "being together," with no agenda or purpose — just enjoying each other's company.

That's what I love most about us. Whether we're talking for hours, walking in comfortable silence, or just sitting side by side, those simple moments with you are my favorite part of every day.

So yes, here's to more adventures, more firsts, and more memories, but more than anything, here's to more *us*.

Acasa
Romanian

How you make me feel in one word?

Acasă.

It's a Romanian word, loosely "at home," that describes a feeling of belonging, beyond just a physical place.

A place where you feel comfortable. A place where you feel safe. A place where you feel loved.

For some, it's the house where they grew up. For others, it's a favorite café or a quiet corner of the world. But for me?

It's wherever you are.

"Love is like butter — it's good with bread."

— Yiddish proverb

Tsuki ga kirei desu
Japanese

Did you know that in Japan, the phrase "The moon is beautiful, isn't it?" is a secret way to say I love you?

It's meant to express love indirectly, as directly stating your feelings in Japanese culture can sometimes be considered impolite.

Pronounced "tsuki ga kirei desu", there are three main ways you can respond:

"Shin demo ii wa" (I can die happy)
"Sou desu ne" (It's true, isn't it?)
"Anata mo utsukushii" (So are you)

In our case, though, all three responses are true: I could die happy, the moon is beautiful, and so are you.

Zhi zi zhi shou, yu zi xie lao
Chinese

Some people say love is hard, but I think it's as simple as:

Zhi zi zhi shou, yu zi xie lao.

This age-old Chinese idiom means "hold hands with you, grow old with you."

It speaks to the promise of lifelong love and commitment — to walk through life side by side, no matter what challenges come your way, no matter how time changes you both.

And that is my promise to you: to hold your hand through it all, no matter what.

All over the world

Have you ever felt a longing for something you couldn't put into words?

Hiraeth (Welsh) is a deep yearning for something lost or distant — an ache for a home, a person, or a time that may never return.

Sehnsucht (German) is a deep, almost painful longing for a future you can picture, but can never quite reach.

And *toska* (Russian) is an aching void for something unknown, a feeling of emptiness that tugs at your soul.

None of them have a direct English translation, but they all come close to describing how I felt before I met you.

Manabamate

[Rapa Nui] *noun*

The lack of appetite you experience when falling in love, unique to the aboriginal Polynesian inhabitants of Easter Island.

Kummerspeck

[German] *noun*

The excess weight gained from emotional eating during heartbreak. Literally "grief bacon."

Vacilando
Spanish

I used to worry about where my life was heading.

Was I on the right path? Were the pieces falling into place? Would I ever figure it all out?

But then I met you, and suddenly, the destination didn't seem so important anymore. That's when I realized something...

Vacilando is a Spanish word that means to wander or travel, knowing the journey itself is more important than the destination.

Now, on this journey of life, the questions that once weighed on me have faded away. The doubts, the fears, the endless 'what-ifs' — they've all been replaced by a sense of calm and certainty.

Because with you by my side, I know we can conquer anything. With you by my side, every path feels like the right one. With you, it's not about the destination, but about embracing every beautiful twist and turn along the way.

So, where to next?

Vivre d'amour et d'eau fraîche
French

Wanna know how much I love you?

In French they say *vivre d'amour et d'eau fraîche*, which means "to live on love and fresh water."

It describes the kind of love where nothing else matters, where just being together feels like enough to sustain you.

And for me, it is.

Because if I have you, I have everything I'll ever need.

Njuta

Swedish

The key to happiness?

"Fear less, hope more; eat less, chew more; whine less, breathe more; talk less, say more; love more; and all good things are yours." — Swedish proverb

This is *njuta*, the Swedish art of delighting in life. It's about appreciating what's already there, focusing on what you have, and finding happiness in the simple things.

So I say let's live by those words: let's fear less, hope more; whine less, breathe more; talk less, say more; love more.

The rest will come naturally.

Firgun

[Hebrew] *noun*

The simple, unselfish joy that something good has happened to someone else.

Mamihlapinatapai
Yaghan

You know that moment when you catch each other's eye and it's clear you both want the same thing, but neither of you makes the first move?

The Yaghan people have a word for it — *mamihlapinatapai* — meaning "a look shared by two people who both want to initiate something, but neither will start."

With that in mind, the next time you catch me looking at you, remember this:

Yes, I am thinking what you're thinking.

Sobok sobok

Korean

In Korean, *sobok sobok* is a phrase that describes the beauty of light snow falling and piling up on the ground.

There's no equivalent for it in English, but it literally means "falling falling," which feels fitting, because that's exactly how I fell for you.

Like snowflakes drifting down, your love settled over me until my whole world was blanketed in something soft, bright, and new.

And just like snow, I'm still falling, falling for you each and every day.

Tsavt tanem

Armenian

If you hurt, I hurt. If you struggle, I struggle. That's *tsavt tanem*.

In *Armenian*, tsavt tanem means "let me take your pain." It's a way of saying, "Lean on me. Whatever you're carrying, I'll carry it with you."

That's not just something I say — it's something I live by.

As long as we're together, you'll never have to bear life's burdens alone. Your joys are mine to celebrate, and your struggles are mine to shoulder, always.

"In love there are two things – bodies and words."

— Joyce Carol Oates, American writer

Nunc scio quid sit amor
Latin

Since meeting you, I've learned so many amazing things.

Now, I know how it feels to wake up with a heart full of gratitude.
Now, I know how it feels to be completely safe in someone's arms.
Now, I know what it means to truly share a life with someone.

But most of all, *nunc scio quid sit amor.*

(Now I know what love is; *Latin*)

Estrenar

Spanish

With you, everything feels like the first time; like *estrenar*.

In Spanish, estrenar describes the unique thrill of experiencing something for the first time, whether that be wearing a new outfit, taking a new car for a spin, or opening the pages of an unread book.

For me, estrenar is what it feels like to love you. Even now, I still get butterflies when you smile at me, when your hand brushes mine, or when you say my name.

And the best part? It's not just the first time — it's the *last* time.

Because with you, I've found my forever.

Nmout alik

Arabic

Love isn't just about words — it's about what you'd be willing to do. And in Arabic, *nmout alik* says it all.

This phrase translates colloquially to "I love you to death" or "I would die for you," but it's often used as a substitute for "I love you" in countries like Algeria and Tunisia.

It may sound a bit intense, but the sentiment is true: I would do absolutely anything for you, and I never want you to forget that.

Fensterln

[German] *verb*

A Bavarian-German word derived from *fenster* (window), describing the tradition of climbing through a lover's window at night to court them in secret.

Gezellig

Dutch

Ask a Dutch person to sum up their culture in one word, and they'll likely say *gezellig*.

It's hard to translate, but easy to feel. A family dinner? Gezellig. Catching up with a friend over coffee? Gezellig. Even a quiet evening on the couch can be gezellig.

At its core, it's about warmth, connection, and being with the people who make life feel full.

And to me?

Talking with you is gezellig. Laughing with you is gezellig. Holding you close is gezellig.

Because what makes a moment gezellig isn't the setting — it's you.

Saudade

Portuguese

Love doesn't always exist in the present. Sometimes, it lingers in the spaces between, felt in memories, in distance, in the ache of something that once was or could have been.

The Portuguese call this *saudade* — a melancholic longing so deep, it carries both sadness and sweetness, absence and presence all at once.

And when I think of you, I feel it too — not because you're far away, but because no amount of time with you will ever feel like enough.

Güzelliğe âşık bir kalp asla yaşlanmaz
Turkish

There's an ancient Turkish proverb that says, "A heart in love with beauty never grows old."

And when I look at you, I understand why. Because beauty isn't just in what the eyes can see — it's in the kindness you show, the warmth of your presence, the way your love fills every space it touches.

So even as the years pass, and even as time changes everything else, one thing will never fade: my love for you. That much I know.

"Beauty is simply reality seen with the eyes of love."

— Rabindranath Tagore, Indian Bengali polymath

I've said a lot in this book — used many words, made a lot of promises — but I ask only one thing of you in return:

Aime-moi, s'il te plaît (French)

Aishite kudasai (Japanese)

Ama-me, por favor (Portuguese)

Amami, ti prego (Italian)

Ámame, por favor (Spanish)

Älska mig, snälla (Swedish)

Aroha mai (Māori)

Bitte, liebe mich (German)

Chop chan dai mai (Thai)

Cintaiku, tolong (Indonesian/Malay)

Dua-më, të lutem (Albanian)

Ewedihalehu, bejew (Amharic)

Hibbini, min fadlak (Arabic)

Ik hou van je, alsjeblieft (Dutch)

Kochaj mnie, proszę (Polish)

Ljubavi me, molim te (Serbo-Croatian)

Mahal mo ako, pakiusap (Tagalog)

Miluj mě, prosím (Czech)

Nyoaran oe, tolaha (Rapa Nui)

Oulak anhi, s'il vous plaît (Wolof)

Rakastathan minua (Finnish)

Saranghae juseyo (Korean)

Se parakalo, agapame (Greek)

Tinqini jekk jogħġbok (Maltese)

Tsavt tanem, khndrem (Armenian)

Uhibbini min fadlik (Arabic)

Voli me, molim te (Serbo-Croatian)

Yêu em/anh đi, làm ơn (Vietnamese)

Zrighkem, min fadlak (Berber/ Tamazight)

Translation: please, love me.

Printed in Great Britain
by Amazon

f7aa1c3b-63ae-4746-9078-e68577b8cd0aR01